LIGHT
Let's Investigate

by Ruth Owen and Victoria Dobney

Published in 2019 by Ruby Tuesday Books Ltd.

Copyright © 2019 Ruby Tuesday Books Ltd.

All rights reserved. No part of this publication may be reproduced in whole or in part, stored in any retrieval system, or transmitted in any form or by any means, electronic, mechanical, photocopying, recording, or otherwise, without written permission from the publisher.

Editor: Mark J. Sachner
Designer: Emma Randall
Production: John Lingham

Photo credits:

Alamy: 9 (top left), 21 (right bottom); Vincent Bal: 22; Creative Commons: 9 (top right); NASA: 5 (centre right), 27 (bottom); Science Photo Library: 17 (top), 29 (bottom right); Shutterstock: Cover, 1, 2—3, 4—5, 6—7, 8, 10—11, 12—13, 14—15, 16, 17 (bottom), 18, 19 (top), 20, 21 (top), 21 (left), 21 (centre right), 24—25, 26—27, 29 (top), 29 (bottom left), 29 (bottom centre), 30—31, 32; Superstock: 15 (top right), 19 (bottom), 28.

ISBN 978-1-78856-042-9

Printed in China by Toppan Leefung Printing Limited

www.rubytuesdaybooks.com

Contents

The download button shows there are free worksheets or other resources available.
Go to:
www.rubytuesdaybooks.com/scienceKS2

What Is Light?

Imagine you are sitting in a dark wardrobe inside a dark room. Everything around you looks black. You can't see the clothes hanging above you or the wardrobe doors.

You can't even see your own hands if you hold them right up to your face. Why?

Your hands, the clothes, the wardrobe doors are all still there, but something important is missing.

Light is a form of **energy** that we can see with our **eyes**.

We need light in order to see the world around us.

Dark is the absence of light.

Just as being absent from school means you're not there, the absence of light means there's no light, and so darkness is created.

Our main **light source** on Earth is the Sun. If you stand in a field in the daytime you can see grass, trees, flowers and thousands of different colours. This is possible because of the Sun's light.

⚠ **WARNING**

You should NEVER look directly at the Sun because it will badly damage your eyes – even if you are wearing sunglasses. Your eyes would act a little like a magnifying glass. They would focus the Sun's powerful, bright light into your eyes and burn them!

The Sun is a **natural source** of light.

Our Super Star

The Sun is a star – just like the thousands of other stars we can see in the night sky. It's a giant ball of gases that creates light and heat. The Sun looks huge in the sky because it's the closest star to Earth.

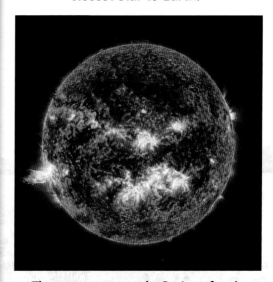

The temperature on the Sun's surface is about 5500°C.

Scientists use spacecraft and special equipment to take photos of the Sun (like this one). Then everyone can safely look at the amazing images.

Keeping Warm

Light from the Sun also heats the Earth. Without this heat, Earth would be too cold for any form of life to live here.

Sources of Light

The Sun is a natural light source. At night, when it's dark, we use streetlights or lamps to light up our world. These light sources are **artificial**, which means they are made by people.

Light travels from one place to another at high speed. The instant a lamp is switched on, light from the lightbulb travels out into the room.

Fire

Fireworks

Stars

Observe & Classify: LIGHT SOURCES

Look at the light sources in the photos. Are they natural or artificial?

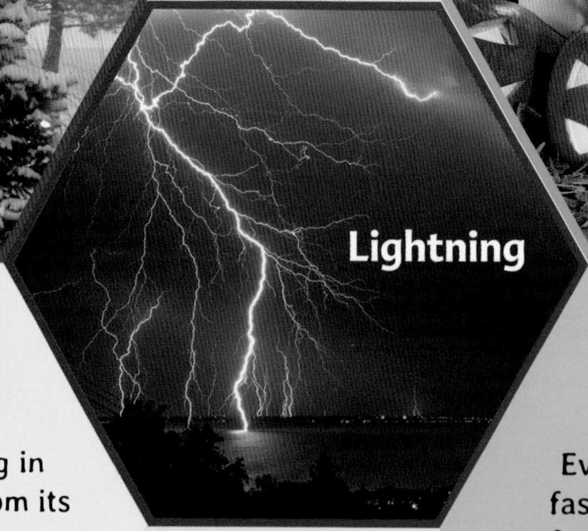

Candles

Fairy lights

Lightning

The Speed of Light

Light is the fastest thing in the universe. It travels from its source at 299,792 kilometres per second. If you could move at this speed, you would be able to zoom around Earth 7.5 times in just one second!

Speedy Sunlight

Even though light travels fast, it takes eight minutes for the Sun's light to reach Earth. That's because the Sun is about 150 million kilometres from the Earth.

What Is Moonlight?

Sometimes at night, the moon is so bright it can help us see in the dark. Unlike the Sun, however, the Moon doesn't make light. The moonlight we see is actually the Sun's light **reflecting** off the Moon.

From Earth a full moon can look like this.

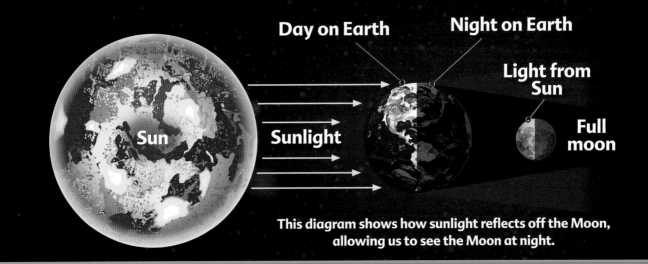

Day on Earth   Night on Earth

Light from Sun

Sun   Sunlight   Full moon

This diagram shows how sunlight reflects off the Moon, allowing us to see the Moon at night.

Let's Investigate

Is it a source of light?

Equipment:
- A notebook and pencil
- A cardboard box with a lid
- A torch (switched on)
- A piece of aluminium foil
- A high-vis vest or jacket
- A tablet (switched on)

Method:

1 With a pencil, carefully pierce a small hole in the side of the cardboard box.

2 Look carefully at these four objects.

Which ones are a source of light?
Write your predictions in your notebook.

3 Close the curtains or blinds in the room. Lower the lights so the room is dim.

4 Place one of your objects inside the box and secure the lid.

5 Look through the small hole you made in the box to see if the object is giving out any light.

6 Record your findings.

7 Repeat for the other three objects and any others that you may wish to test.

Did your results match your predictions?

How Light Reflects

Look around you. What do you see? Walls, floor, the ceiling. Maybe you can see a table or a sofa. These objects are not giving off light but we can still see them. That's because they are reflecting light.

This book is reflecting light RIGHT NOW. The light may be coming from a window or from a lamp or ceiling light. The light in the room is reflecting off the book's pages and into your eyes. This makes it possible for you to see the words and pictures.

Most surfaces or materials reflect light, but they reflect it in different amounts. The smooth, polished surface of a **mirror** reflects almost all the light that hits it. In fact, mirrors reflect light so well you can see yourself in them.

How Do Mirrors Work?

A mirror is made from a thin, clear sheet of glass that's coated on one side with a layer of metal such as aluminium. Light from the room reflects off your face and into the mirror. The mirror reflects the light back into your eyes so well, that you can actually see your face.

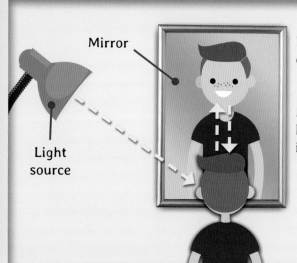

Mirror

Light reflects off face

Mirror reflects light back into eyes

Light source

Surfaces that are not smooth like a mirror do not reflect light well. These surfaces scatter the light or **absorb** it. For example, a carpet only reflects some of the light that hits it. That's why you can't see your face in a carpet!

Good Hair Day?

Look for your reflection in objects around your home or classroom. Which objects are best at reflecting light and what do you notice about them?

The silver light bands on a safety vest do not give off light, but they are made from a material that is very good at reflecting light. It is called retroreflective material.

Staying Safe With Light

Some retroreflective material is made of tiny beads. When a car's headlights shine on the beads, they don't scatter or absorb the light. The beads reflect the light directly back towards the car and into the driver's eyes. The material looks very bright in the dark, but it's not actually giving off light – it's just a very good reflector.

Retroreflective beads seen under a microscope

Let's Investigate

How well does it reflect light?

Equipment:
- A notebook and pen
- A torch
- A mirror
- A piece of smooth aluminium foil
- A crumpled piece of aluminium foil
- A blank wall

Method:

Look at the mirror, pieces of foil and wall. Which do you think will reflect light best? Write your predictions in your notebook.

1 Place the mirror securely on a table.

2 Close the curtains or blinds in the room. Lower the lights so the room is dim.

3 Shine your torch into the mirror at an angle.

Is the beam of light reflected well? How can you tell? Record your findings.

4 Next, repeat the activity with a smooth piece of foil and record your results.

5 Repeat again with the crumpled foil and then with the wall and record your results.

Was one material better at reflecting light than the others? Why do you think that was?

Got to Get Through This!

Light is able to shine through some materials but not others. Materials that let light through are **transparent**, or see-through.

Glass and some objects made of plastic are transparent.

Let's Test It

If it's daytime, look out of a window. What do you see? You can see objects outside because the Sun's light is reflecting off them. Then the light is travelling through the transparent glass into your eyes.

Some materials allow just a small amount of light to shine through them. These materials are **translucent**.

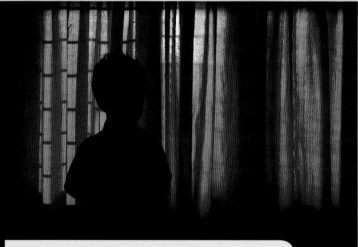

These curtains are translucent. We can't see the outside world through them, but they still let some light into the room.

Materials that block all light are **opaque**. These materials don't allow any light to pass through.

This suitcase is opaque. That's why we can't see what's inside.

You Are Opaque!

Place your hand over this page. Now you can't see some of the words and pictures. Your opaque hand is blocking the light that's reflecting off the page and stopping it reaching your eyes.

Let's Talk!

Describe the different parts of the car using the words and phrases below:

- shine through
- light source
- translucent
- transparent
- opaque
- not shine through

Materials and Properties

Being transparent, translucent or opaque is one of a material's **properties**. A material's properties make it a good or bad choice to do a certain job. For example, a sheet of opaque cardboard would be useless for making a car windscreen. And transparent wrapping paper would take all the fun out of opening a present!

Let's Investigate

Is it transparent, translucent or opaque?

Equipment:
- A notebook and pen
- A torch
- 15 cm x 15 cm square pieces of the following materials:
  - Plastic (from a sandwich bag)
  - Coloured tissue paper
  - Cardboard
  - Aluminium foil
  - Tracing paper

Method:

1 Predict whether you think each material is opaque, translucent or transparent. Record your predictions in your notebook.

2 Close the curtains or blinds in the room. Lower the lights so the room is dim.

3 Hold up one of the squares of material about 15 cm from the wall. Turn on the torch and shine it on the material.

4 Record if the material lets the light shine through onto the wall, shine through onto the wall faintly or not shine through at all.

Is the material opaque, translucent or transparent? Record your results.

5 Repeat with all the squares of material and record your results.

Did your predictions match what you observed?

Making Shadows

When the light from a light source is blocked by an opaque object, what happens?

When light is blocked, a **shadow** forms. A shadow is a dark area where the light cannot reach. The shadow is the same shape as the opaque object that blocked the light.

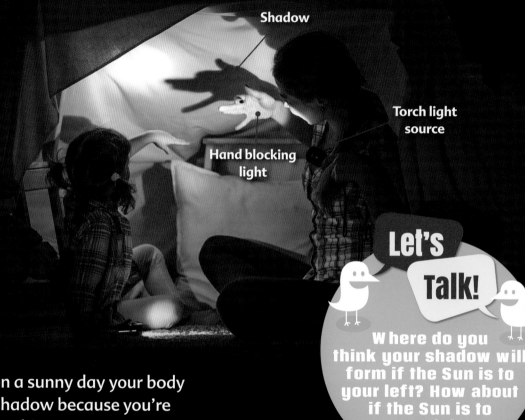

Shadow

Torch light source

Hand blocking light

Let's Talk!

Where do you think your shadow will form if the Sun is to your left? How about if the Sun is to your right?

Outside on a sunny day your body makes a shadow because you're an opaque object.

If the Sun is **behind** you, your body blocks some of the light and a shadow forms in front of you.

If the Sun is **in front** of you, your shadow will form **behind** you.

Let's Investigate

Have you ever noticed that sometimes objects form huge shadows? But at other times an object's shadow is only small. Let's discover why this happens.

Can you make the shadows the right size?

Download our silhouette resources (as below) and try to make a scene with the shadows in the correct proportion. How will you make the cat smaller than the child? How will you make the car bigger than the bird?

Equipment:
- Silhouette worksheets
- Scissors
- Lolly sticks
- Sticky tape
- A lamp or a torch
- A helper

Method:

1. Print off the silhouette worksheets and carefully cut around each image.

2. Using sticky tape, stick each image onto a lolly stick to make puppets.

3. Close the curtains or blinds in the room. Lower the lights so the room is dim.

4. Turn on a light source (a lamp or torch) and point it at a blank wall.

5. With your helper hold up the puppets between the light source and the wall.

6. Move the puppets closer and further away from the light source until the shadows are in the correct proportion.

Can you think of a rule to be successful with this task? To make the puppet's shadow smaller, you need to move it _____ the light source.

How Does Light Travel?

When light is produced by a light source, such as the Sun, a torch or a candle, how does it travel?

Light travels in straight lines.

When light reaches a transparent object, like a window, it passes through and keeps on going straight.

When light reaches a mirror, it reflects off the mirror's highly reflective surface and keeps on going straight.

When light reaches an opaque object it can't go around it. The light that was heading directly for the object is blocked and the object casts a shadow.

However, the light above, below and on either side of the opaque object keeps travelling in straight lines.

Light travels through the air in straight lines at high speed. However, when light hits water, it slows down. As the light slows, it **refracts**, or bends and changes direction.

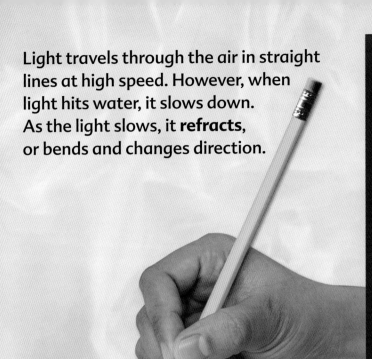

Refraction In Action

When you hold a pencil and look at it, the light reflected by the pencil is travelling in straight lines through the air to your eyes. When part of the pencil is put into water, the light it is reflecting slows and refracts. This makes the underwater part of the pencil look different to the part that's in the air.

The refraction of the light makes the pencil look as if it's broken or bending.

Let's Revise

The Sun

1 Light travels in straight lines.

2 Light reflects off objects.

3 Your eyes capture the reflected light, and you see the sunflowers.

How Do We See?

Your eyes are incredible organs that are designed to capture light and allow you to see.

The pupil looks black but it's actually a small, round opening.

The white part of your eye is a tough, outer covering called the sclera.

The round coloured part of your eye is called the iris.

Your Eyes in Action

1 Each eye is covered with a see-through, dome-shaped layer of **tissue** called the **cornea**. The cornea captures light and directs it into the pupil.

2 Once the light is inside your eye it hits another see-through part called the **lens**.

3 The lens focuses the light onto the **retina** at the back of the eyeball.

Each of your retinas contains millions of tiny **cells** called rods and cones.

4 The light hits the rods and cones. They collect information from the light and use it to create a picture.

Let's Talk!

Once your eyes have made a picture, another organ in your body helps you to see it. Which organ do you think that is?

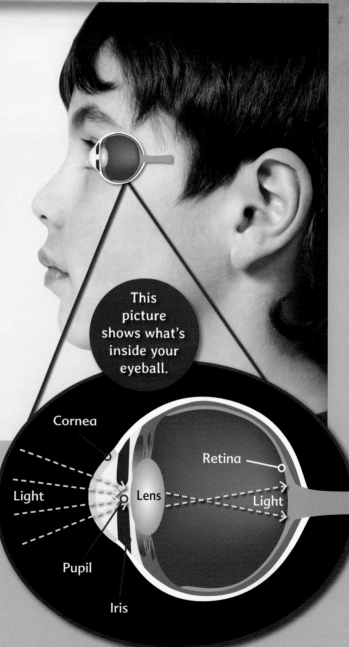

This picture shows what's inside your eyeball.

Cornea

Retina

Light

Lens

Light

Pupil

Iris

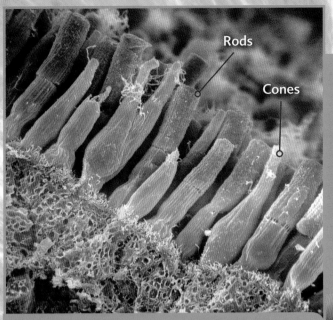

Rods

Cones

A section of a retina seen under a microscope.

Rods and Cones

There are about 120 million rods in each of your retinas. They detect black, white, grey and the shapes of things. They also help you to see in dim light. Each retina also contains about 7 million cones. The cones detect colours, but they do not work well in dim light.

Your eyes can see about 10 million different colours.

Let's Investigate

Can you see colours in dim light?

Equipment:
- A notebook and pen
- 6 pieces of coloured paper
- A black marker pen
- A watch or phone for timing

STOPWATCH

Method:

Look at the six colours. How many do you think you will be able to identify in dim light? Write your prediction in your notebook.

1 Close the curtains or blinds in a room. Turn off or lower the lights so the room is very dim and you can only just see.

2 Wait for about five minutes to allow your eyes to get used to the dim light.

3 Look at the six pieces of paper.

Can you tell what colour each piece of paper is? You can write your answer on the paper.

4 Turn on the lights.

Did your prediction match what happened? If not, why do you think this is?

(The answers are at the bottom of the page.)

ANSWERS: In dim light, the rod cells still allowed you to see the pieces of paper. However, you could not see the colours well because cone cells do not work in dim light.

Eyes + Brain = Sight

The rods and cones in your retinas produce a picture using light. However, the picture that's created is actually upside down!

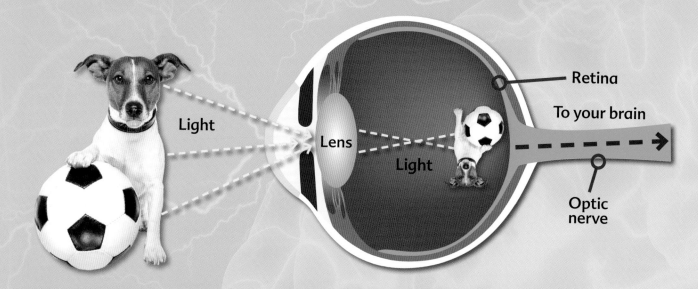

Light

Lens

Light

Retina

To your brain

Optic nerve

What happens next?

The upside down picture speeds along your **optic nerves.** The optic nerve in each eye is like a cable connecting the retina to your brain.

When your brain receives the picture, it flips it the right way up. Then it figures out what the picture shows and in an instant you see the object you were looking at.

When you look at an object each of your eyes gets a slightly different view. Your brain combines the two views into one picture.

Brain

POP CORN

Too Much or Too Little Light?

If the light around you is very bright, your pupils get smaller to protect your eyes from too much light entering them. If there is not enough light, your pupils dilate, or get bigger, to let in as much light as possible. Tiny muscles in your irises make your pupils bigger or smaller.

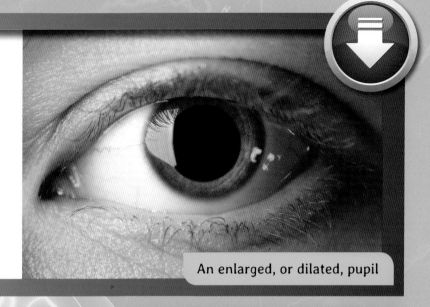

An enlarged, or dilated, pupil

The Eye Protection Squad

Your precious eyes have lots of protection.

Each eye has a hairy eyebrow that directs sweat, soapy water and other moisture to the sides of your face away from your eyes.

Your eyes are inside bony sockets in your skull to protect them.

Our eyelids can instantly snap shut to keep out strong light and harmful objects.

Your eyelashes catch dust and tiny bits of debris before they get into your eyes.

Tears made of water, salt, oil, slimy mucus and germ-killing chemicals wash away debris that could harm or irritate our eyes.

Each blink spreads a tiny quantity of tears around your eyes to clean them and stop them drying out.

We blink about **15 to 20 times** each minute. Like breathing, **blinking** is something our bodies do **automatically** but we can also **control** it if we like.

More Shadow Science

Go outside on a sunny day and you will soon spot your own shadow. But have you noticed that sometimes your shadow is short and at other times it looks very long and stretched?

Why do shadows get longer and shorter?

The length of shadows is all to do with the position of the Sun in the sky, or the position of a light source such as a torch.

When the Sun is low in the sky in the morning and late afternoon, objects (including you) block more sunlight. This makes an object's shadow grow longer.

By midday, when the Sun is directly above an object, less light is blocked. This creates a shorter shadow.

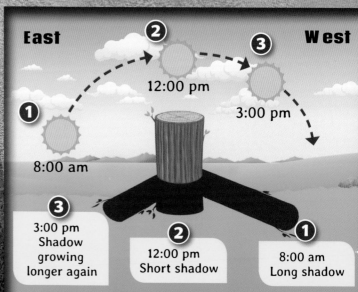

East • West
2 12:00 pm
1 8:00 am
3 3:00 pm

3 3:00 pm Shadow growing longer again
2 12:00 pm Short shadow
1 8:00 am Long shadow

Earth and Sun Mind-Boggler

Every day it looks as if the Sun is travelling across the sky, but actually it's Earth that's moving! As Earth rotates, or spins, your part of the world changes its position in relation to the Sun. As Earth spins it makes it look as if the Sun rises in the east, moves through the sky and sets again in the west.

Night – The Biggest Shadow Of All

During daytime the place where you live faces the Sun. But each day, as Earth rotates, your part of the world eventually spins away from the Sun's light and into darkness. When night falls it's because we're inside the giant shadow that's created by Earth blocking the Sun's light.

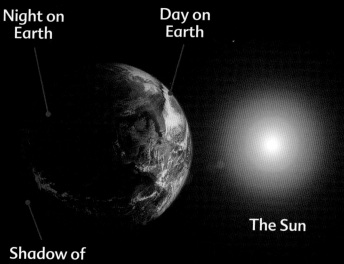

Night on Earth

Day on Earth

Shadow of Earth

The Sun

Shadow Time

The position of shadows can be used to tell the time. A sundial is an instrument that's marked with the hours of the day. As the Sun's position changes in the sky, the shadow cast by the sundial's pointer lands on the number for that time of day.

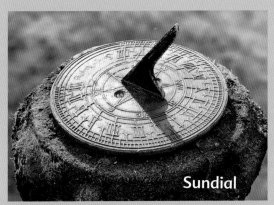

Sundial

It's possible to make a simple sundial just with a stick and some pebbles.

Let's Talk!

How do you think the shadow formed in the picture below?

What do you think is making the shadow on the hillside?

ANSWERS: A person onboard a plane took the photograph. The plane is blocking the Sun's light and forming a shadow on the trees. The shadow on the hillside is made by a cloud in the sky. The cloud is blocking the Sun's light.

Swapping Sketches for Shadows

Not all artists use paints or pens. Some use light and shadows in their work.

The absence of light can create impressive illusions, but it requires creativity and patience to make art in this way. Using translucent and opaque objects can bring life and depth to static artwork.

Shadowology

Vincent Bal is a "shadowologist" and filmmaker from Belgium. He adds doodles to the shadows of everyday objects to create imaginative pieces of art. Vincent draws his inspiration from everyday objects and shares his creations on social media.

Hippo-Hop Hipster

The object and the shadow are both important to the final piece.

Blue Bottleache

In this image a translucent object is used to make a different kind of shadow.

Let's Experiment

Make a Shadow Finger Person

Equipment:
- A light source (a torch or lamp)
- A pencil
- Pieces of white paper
- A partner

Method:

1 Close the blinds or curtains in a room and turn off or lower the lights.

2 Put your finger between the light source and the piece of paper (you might need a partner to hold your light source). Experiment with moving it backwards and forwards to create a well-defined shadow.

3 Draw a face and arms on your paper using the shadow as an outline of a person.

4 Take your finger away. Can you or your partner then reposition a finger correctly between your light source and the paper to recreate your character?

Everyday Objects Shadow Sketch

Equipment:
- A light source (a torch or lamp)
- A pencil or pen
- Your choice of objects
- Large sheets of white paper

Method:

1 Close the blinds or curtains in a room and turn off or lower the lights.

2 Think about how Vincent Bal created the shadows in Hippo-Hop Hipster or Blue Bottleache.

3 Place your objects on the paper and experiment with your light source to see what kinds of shadows you can create.

Do the shapes of the shadows remind you of something else? For example, Vincent's hippo shadows looked like hands and arms.

4 Once you have created a shadow you like, draw your picture around and inside the shadow. Finally, give the artwork a name.

Making Rainbows

It's raining. Then the Sun shines. And suddenly . . . Wow!
A colourful **rainbow** is arching across the sky. But without light,
this beautiful weather phenomenon would not be possible.

The ingredients that make a rainbow are:

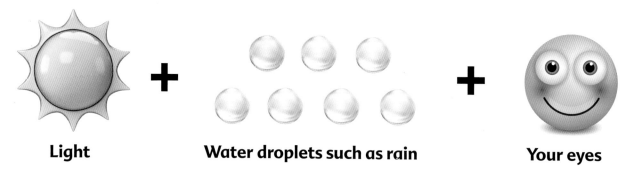

Light + **Water droplets such as rain** + **Your eyes**

The colours in a rainbow actually come from light. A beam of sunlight or the light
from a torch may not look colourful, but it is made up of seven different colours.

Red	Orange	Yellow	Green	Blue	Indigo	Violet

How a Rainbow Forms

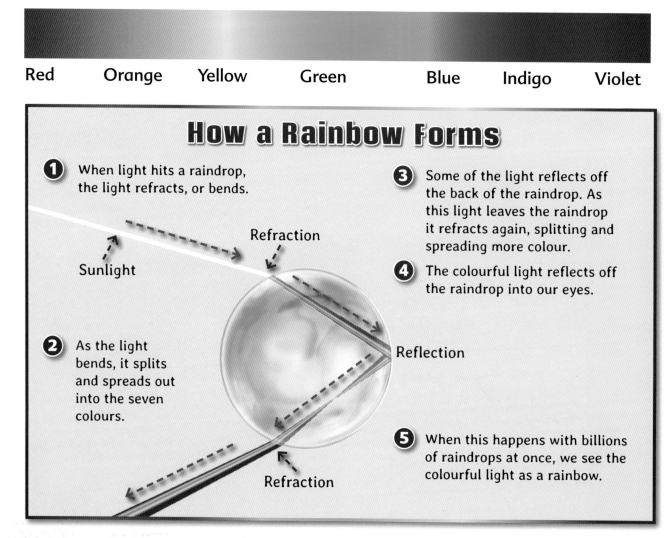

1 When light hits a raindrop, the light refracts, or bends.

2 As the light bends, it splits and spreads out into the seven colours.

3 Some of the light reflects off the back of the raindrop. As this light leaves the raindrop it refracts again, splitting and spreading more colour.

4 The colourful light reflects off the raindrop into our eyes.

5 When this happens with billions of raindrops at once, we see the colourful light as a rainbow.

Refraction

Sunlight

Reflection

Refraction

How to See a Rainbow

Why don't we see more rainbows? It's tricky stuff, but a rainbow isn't actually a thing. It's a trick of the light that only happens if you are in just the right position to see it.

The colours in a rainbow may mix and blur a little, but often it's possible to see the seven colours.

To see a rainbow the Sun must be behind you. The water source, such as rain, mist, a waterfall or spray from a garden hose, must be in front of you. Then if the light hits the water droplets and reflects off them at just the right angle, you will see a rainbow.

Let's Talk!

R O Y G B I V
Make up a saying or sentence that will help someone remember the order of the colours of the rainbow.

Let's Investigate

Can you make a rainbow?

Equipment:
- A large white sheet of paper
- A plain wall
- A torch (with a strong, direct light beam)
- A glass (with no pattern on it)
- A small mirror (that will fit in the glass)
- A jug of water
- A notebook and pen

Method:

1 Look carefully at the equipment.

How do you think some or all of these objects could be used to create a rainbow?

2 Write down your ideas and a method for an experiment.

3 Now try making a rainbow following your method.

4 Record your results.

Was your experiment successful? If so, what colours did you see?

If your ideas didn't work, think about what you can do differently. Write down your new ideas and try again!

Why Is the Sky Blue?

The answer to that question is . . .

Yes, you guessed it.

Light!

To understand how light makes the sky blue, we need to take a look at Earth's **atmosphere**. The atmosphere is a layer of gases that surrounds our planet.

The atmosphere is made up of tiny floating **molecules** that are too small to see. Most of the molecules are gases.

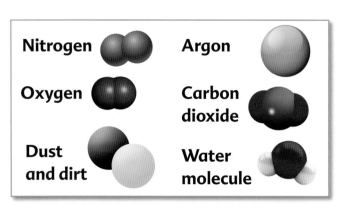

Nitrogen

Oxygen

Dust and dirt

Argon

Carbon dioxide

Water molecule

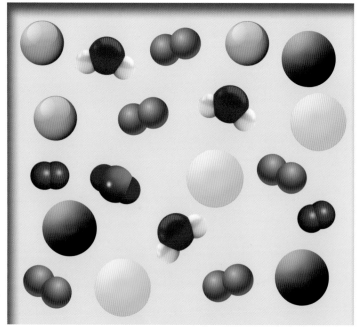

Tiny molecules of water also float in the atmosphere. So do particles of dust and dirt.

When light from the Sun shines through Earth's atmosphere, it bumps into all the tiny floating molecules. The light gets bounced and scattered in all directions.

The blue light gets scattered the most and makes the sky look blue.

The atmosphere reaches up to about 120 kilometres above Earth's surface. From space, it's possible to see Earth's atmosphere.

Atmosphere

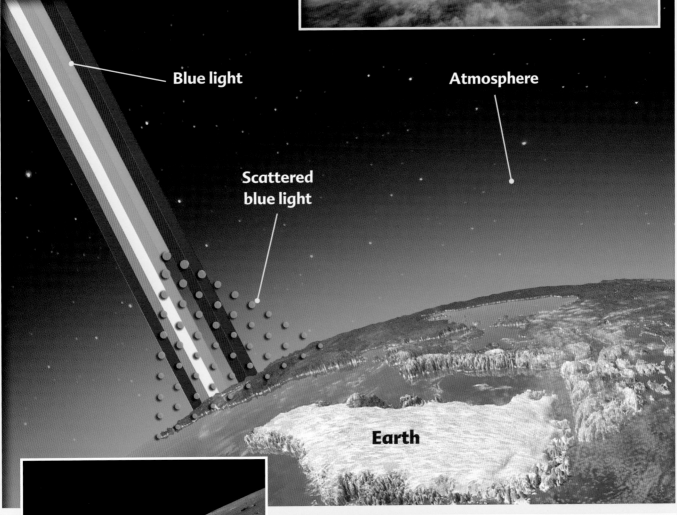

Blue light

Atmosphere

Scattered blue light

Earth

A Black Sky

If Earth had no atmosphere, the sky would look black – day and night! That's because there would be no atmosphere scattering the blue light. The planet Mercury has no atmosphere, so its sky is always black.

This image of Mercury's surface was taken by a robotic spacecraft called MESSENGER that visited the planet.

Animal Kingdom Light

It's not only the Sun, fire or lightning that are natural light sources. Some animals are, too! The light that's created by animals is called bioluminescence.

In a dark world, deep below the ocean's surface, a small light moves through the black water. A little fish is drawn to the light. Could it be food?

Suddenly, an enormous mouth of razor-sharp teeth appears from the gloom beneath the light. The fish has just been lured to its death by an anglerfish!

Anglerfish get their name because, like human anglers, they use a fishing rod-like body part to catch squid, shrimp and other fish. This body part is called a **lure**.

Lure (light)

A Glowing Fishing Rod

The light in an anglerfish's lure is made by **bacteria** that produce their own light. The bacteria live in the lure and get **nutrients** from the fish. In return, the fish uses the bacteria's bioluminescence to catch its prey.

An anglerfish

Glow-worm

Lighting Up the Night

As night fell this female glow-worm crawled from her underground burrow. She climbed up a grass stem. Then she produced a yellowish-green light to attract a mate. The light is produced when chemicals in her abdomen mix with oxygen.

Beetle Bioluminescence

Glow-worms are actually beetles. There are hundreds of different types of beetles that use bioluminescence to attract mates. In some types the female lights up. In others it's the males that produce light.

Bioluminescence

Abdomen

Bee Vision

Scientists call the light that humans see "visible light" because it can be seen by our eyes. However, there are also other kinds of light. Some animals, such as bees, can see ultraviolet light. Many flowers have patterns to attract insects that can only be seen in ultraviolet light.

To human eyes, these flowers look yellow with a black centre.

In ultraviolet light, a bee sees a dark pattern on the petals that guides it to the flower's centre to collect nectar and pollen.

Glossary

absorb
To take in or soak up.

artificial
Made by humans; not natural.

atmosphere
A layer of gases surrounding a planet, moon or star.

bacteria
Microscopic living things. Some bacteria are helpful, while others (known as germs) can cause disease.

bioluminescence
Natural light that's produced by a living thing, such as an insect or fish.

cell
A very tiny part of a living thing. Bones, muscles, eyes and every part of you are made of cells.

cornea
A see-through, dome-shaped layer of tissue that covers your iris and pupil. The cornea captures light and directs it into your eye.

energy
The force that allows things to move and happen. There are different types of energy, such as light energy and electrical energy.

eye
An organ in the body of a person or animal that is used for sight.

lens
A see-through part of your eye that focuses light onto the retina.

light source
A means of producing light, such as the Sun or fire (natural light sources) or lamps and torches (artificial, or humanmade, light sources).

lure
Something used to attract prey.

mirror
A surface, usually made of glass, which reflects light so well it can reflect a clear image.

molecule
A group of atoms that are bonded together. For example, a water molecule (H_2O) is made of two hydrogen atoms and one oxygen atom. Everything is made of atoms and they are the smallest particles of any object or substance.

nutrients
Substances needed by a plant or animal to help it live and grow. Vitamins and minerals such as calcium and potassium are all nutrients.

opaque
Able to completely block light; not transparent. For example, a brick wall is opaque.

optic nerve
A cable-like group of cells that carry information from the retina in your eye to your brain.

organ
A part of the body that has a particular job to do.

property
A quality that helps to describe what a material or substance is like — for example, transparent or opaque, hard or soft, shiny or dull.

pupil
A small, round opening in the centre of your eye that allows light to enter.

rainbow
A colourful, arch-like natural phenomenon caused by light refracting and reflecting off water drops, such as rain.

reflect
To throw back and not absorb. For example, a mirror reflects, or throws back, light.

refract
To bend light, or make it change direction.

retina
The area at the back of your eye that takes light and turns it into a picture that's sent to the brain.

shadow
A dark area or shape that's produced when an opaque object blocks light from a light source.

surface
The outside part or uppermost (top) layer of something.

tissue
A group of connected cells in your body that work together. Cells are very tiny parts of a living thing.

translucent
Semi-transparent and able to let some light pass through. For example, a thin, plastic carrier bag is translucent.

transparent
See-through and able to let light through. For example, a glass window is transparent.

Index